In memory of Rosemary Canter
with deep thanks for all you did for me

Princess Pearl: A Friend to Treasure
First published in 2012 by Hodder Children's Books
Princess Pearl: A Friend to Treasure © Emma Thomson 2012

Hodder Children's Books, 338 Euston Road, London, NW1 3BH
Hodder Children's Books Australia, Level 17/207 Kent Street, Sydney, NSW 2000

The right of Emma Thomson to be identified as the author and
illustrator of this Work has been asserted by her in accordance with
the Copyright, Designs and Patents Act 1988.

A catalogue record of this book is available from the British Library.

ISBN 9781 444 90584 7

Printed in China

Hodder Children's Books is a division of Hachette Children's Books.
An Hachette UK Company.
www.hachette.co.uk

A division of Hachette Children's Books

# Princess Pearl

## A Friend to Treasure

Emma Thomson

*I*T WAS A WINDY DAY. Pearl searched in
the cupboard for something warm to
wrap up in. As she pushed through rows of
clothes, she suddenly tumbled forward…

…and found herself in the Underwater Kingdom! It was eerily quiet. There was not a single princess to greet her.

"Hello! Is anyone there?" called Pearl into the distance.

On the crest of the waves, she could hear faint voices. Pearl followed the noise…

$S$he soon found what was keeping her friends!

"Oh Pearl, thank goodness you are here," cried Princess Citrine. "Coral Princess Velvet was swept here on a tidal wave all the way from our enemies in the Reef Kingdom. What shall we do? She's badly hurt."

"It doesn't matter who she is, she needs our care and plenty of rest," said Pearl, taking charge.

$T$he princesses set to work, nursing the poorly princess back to health. They fed her the best food in the kingdom. They put special ointment on her cuts and bruises.

But even though the cuts started to heal, Princess Velvet would not open her eyes.

"She must be homesick," whispered Pearl. "She's not well enough to travel home yet, but maybe we could read her stories and bring home to her!"

"*B*ut she won't understand," said Princess Sapphire kindly. "She speaks a different language."

"That doesn't matter. She'll hear friendship in my voice," insisted Pearl.

So, hour by hour, day after day, Pearl read Velvet stories about the Reef Kingdom and collected exotic corals to decorate her room.

"Why don't you open your eyes," offered Pearl. "Then you'll be able to go home."

Very slowly and very carefully, Princess Velvet's lashes lifted. "I was afraid to open them as Coral Princesses' eyes can turn enemies to stone."

"We are not your enemy; we are your friends," said Pearl, hugging her tightly. "Let's take you home."

The next day, Pearl and Velvet arrived at the Reef Kingdom.

"Please accept this pearl as a token of our friendship," said the Coral Princesses with open eyes. They were delighted to have Princess Velvet home at last.

As Pearl said goodbye to Velvet she disappeared through a coral archway…

…and found herself back in the cupboard.

"True friends are never far apart," she said,
holding the coral pearl close to her heart.